FAST
CHEAP
&
SKINNY

FAST
CHEAP
&
SKINNY

Written and Illustrated

by

L.P.B. Reinhart and M.K. Streeter

WIENER DOG PRESS
A division of Coe House Publishing
San Jose, California

ISBN 0-962978-0-4

SECOND PRINTING

Table of Contents

Why Cook At All?

No matter how you try to avoid it, there are times when it boils down to cook or starve. Things happen.

You fall in love.

You start staying home more.

You buy a house.

You have children. Children need something more than Frosted Flakes from time to time.

Even Chinese takeout doesn't cut it after a while.

And when you're falling in love, buying a house, having children or just trying to make the rent, you have better things to do with your money than pay three bucks apiece for shrimp you swallow whole standing at the sink.

This is a cookbook for people who cook because they want to eat well or feed somebody well, but don't have the time, energy or interest to pursue the perfect duck mousse.

FAST, CHEAP & SKINNY recipes are all extremely fast, almost embarrassingly easy, and can be made from stuff you already have or can get anywhere, anytime.

They're meals you can make with one pot and half a brain while the other half reads the mail, answers the phone and gets the kids in the tub.

They range from sort of lowfat to super lean. And they're meals your friends, lovers, kids, spouses and internationally famous party guests will love.

Nothing has to be measured carefully or blanched or braised or thickened or scalded. You don't need a food processor, pasta maker, double boiler or linen tea towels.

You may even find you never need another cookbook.

Equipping the Minimal Kitchen

■

Hey, there could be a hundred reasons you're thinking about kitchen equipment right now.

You've taken the dog and moved into a trailer in Puckerbrush, Nevada.

Your parents finally threw you out.

You want your weekend place to reflect a certain Zen.

You're acting out some Martha Stewart backlash feelings.

Your ex-spouse took everything.

You do not wish to clutter your aura with double boilers, ramekins and cheesecake molds.

Or maybe you don't know what a ramekin is and don't care.

Point is, you really don't need much. Whether you're starting from scratch, starting over or streamlining, here is our list of the essentials. The right stuff, as it were:

Blender. Three speeds are plenty, with a glass bending jar instead of plastic—unless you don't care, in which case we don't, either.

Butler's Friend. The cheapest, easiest, best kind of wine bottle opener ever.

ATTRACTIVE COLANDER

Chili pot. Cast iron or oven-proof pot with tight lid, big enough for a whole chicken.

Colander. Something that looks good enough to serve in, too.

Cutting knives. A set of those laser-sharpened ones, including steak knives, will do everything.

Giant Bowl. Glass or crockery.

Large skillet with lid. Black cast iron skillet* with tight-fitting lid, preferably glass so you can see what's happening to your food.

Microwave. It doesn't have to rotate, it doesn't have to be big, but if you don't have one, *get* one. Now.

Nesting Pyrex™ measuring cups. Two or three will do.

Pasta pot. A kettle big enough to cook a grunch of pasta.

Salad bowl. Wooden, preferably teak.*

Salad Spinner. You probably won't be washing salad greens far enough ahead to dry without the help of a spinner.

Saucepan with lid. Not small, not huge.

Spatula. Wooden-handle pancake flipper. This may have to be a garage sale item. Plastic handles tend to melt when accidentally left on the burner.

Spoons. Serving spoons, larger than soup spoons. A slotted spoon is also handy.

NESTING GLASS MEASURING CUPS

---

* *Clean with hot water only. No soap, ever. You knew that, but we felt compelled to remind you.*

Pantry Checklist

The idea is to stay out of the grocery store.

Go once a week or order from a delivery service and don't go at all. Your life will improve. You'll save money. You won't buy those magazines at the checkout counter. You won't run into people you feel obligated to talk to even though you're late and tired and hungry.

Keep your freezer and your cupboards stocked with these indispensables, bought in large enough quantities, and you'll never be without something swell to eat.

Organized according to the way most grocery stores stock their shelves:

■ **Baking Goods section**

Artificial sweetener (Equal™ is our favorite)
Basil
Butter flavor powder (Butter Buds™ or Molly McButter™)
Cinnamon
Cocoa, unsweetened
Lowfat Cooking Spray
Curry powder
Garlic powder
Lemon pepper
Nutmeg
Oregano

Pancake mix, lowfat, "complete"
Parsley
Pepper (coarse grind and regular)
Salt
Tarragon
Thyme

■ Salad Dressings aisle

Lemon juice, bottled (or fresh lemons)
Canola oil or equivalent vegetable oil
Olive oil (darker "virgin" or "extra virgin")
Sesame oil

■ Puddings, Instant Drinks section

Canned milk
Non-fat dry milk

■ Jellies & Jams section

Peanut butter
Old-fashioned oatmeal

■ Canned Foods

Chicken
Clams
Crab
Green beans, short-cut

Green beans, long–cut
Pineapple, crushed, slices or chunks,
unsweetened
Pinto beans
Pumpkin
Stewed tomatoes
Tuna

■ **International Foods**

Pasta (angel hair, egg noodles, linguine, shells,
spaghetti)
Refried Beans
Salsa
Spaghetti sauce
Tomato paste
Tomato sauce
Rice
Soy sauce

■ **Meat counter**
Pork chops
Skinned and boned chicken breasts

■ **Deli/Dairy case**

Capers
Cheese
        Cheddar
        Feta
        Lowfat white cheese such as Mozzarella
        Parmesan or Romano
        Ricotta

Non-fat, plain yogurt
Eggs
Sizzlean™
Turkey sausage link, smoked
Turkey breast, smoked or regular

■ Produce

Apples
Carrots
Celery
Fresh garlic
Mushrooms
Onions
Oranges
Pears
Potatoes
Tomatoes

■ Frozen Foods

Artificial crab
Blackberries
Cherries
Raspberries
Strawberries
Fordhook lima beans
Lowfat ice cream or frozen yogurt
Lowfat pound cake
Peas
Turkey, ground

FROZEN FOODS

MAINSTAYS

Most folks don't really, truly care to eat
something different and amazing every
day of the year. Your Nancy Reagans
and Ivana Trumps aside, most of us
manage without smoked hummingbird
tongue or fois gras except on occasion.

The rest of the time we take a certain
comfort in *familiar* food. And the nifty
thing is—what is almost *too* familiar to
you may be quite exotic to your guests.

Here, then, are some extremely reliable
one-dish meals you can toss together
for yourself, your kids or company. Of
course with company you'll want to
use plates and things. And hide the
cans. And pull out the block of
Parmesan to grate at the table instead
of using pre-fab flakes.

Anticipation rises as the children eagerly await the evening meal.

Eggplant Parmesan

There are people who won't eat eggplant on principle. We try not to invite them to our dinner parties. Everyone else loves this.

Lowfat cooking spray
1 eggplant, sliced in 1/4" slabs
Spaghetti sauce
Mild white cheese

1 Spray cookie sheet with cooking spray.

2 Slice eggplant (the thinner the slice, the faster it cooks), then put one layer eggplant on cookie sheet.

3 Spread your favorite home–made or prepared spaghetti sauce over each piece.

4 Slice or grate cheese over each slice. (Pare fat and calories by using low-cal spaghetti sauce and low-fat cheese.)

5 Bake at 350–400° till eggplant is tender (no resistance when you stick a fork in), about 20 minutes.

Serve with your perennial salad, character bread and/or pasta.

Salade Chinoise

Salade Chinoise sounds niftier somehow than Hot Turkey Salad. Truly delish enough even for snooty foodie types. Makes a generous single serving, so multiply accordingly.

1/4 lb frozen ground turkey
1 Tbsp sesame oil
Half bag frozen stir-fry veggies
1/4 head of head lettuce, sliced
Lite soy sauce
Garlic powder
Blop of rice vinegar
Blop of crunchy peanut butter

1 In a skillet or wok, stir–fry turkey with sesame oil (as much or as little as conscience allows) until turkey is no longer pink.

2 Add frozen veggies to turkey and continue stir frying on high heat till almost tender.

3 Add lettuce and remaining ingredients; stir till heated through.

Serve a la carte or over rice. For those foodie guests, complement with an impertinent little Gewürztraminer.

Uncrab Salad

Substitute artificial crab meat in a classic tuna salad, get this tailgate-party caliber luncheon item, and move your tail on out of the kitchen.

Artificial crab meat (fresh, frozen or canned)
Lowfat mayo
Chopped celery
Lemon pepper
Salt
Chopped apple (optional)
Frozen peas (optional)

1 Stir all ingredients together in a bowl, adjusting seasonings to taste.

2 Serve on lettuce or soft French rolls.

For instant pasta salad, add leftover cold pasta to Uncrab Salad, mix and add more mayo if need be.

Cabbage 'n' Turkey Sausage

If you're a morning person, do this in a crock pot so it's ready when you walk in the door. But if that kind of forethought doesn't come naturally, this dish can be slapped together and ready in 20 minutes. Plus, it can just sit in the pot till your hair is dry, your show is finished or your company arrives.

1 pkg smoked turkey link sausage
1 onion, peeled and halved
4 small potatoes, washed and halved
1 head cabbage, whacked up
1 or 2 apples, quartered
1/2 c water
Salt, pepper

In the crockpot, layer the ingredients, except for water, in the order given, and cook 6-8 hours on low, —OR—

1 On the stove, cut sausage into serving-size lengths and brown in deep-sided large pot.

2 Add onion, potatoes, cabbage, apples and water. Cover tightly.

3 Cook on medium-low heat until cabbage begins to shrink and potatoes are tender. Salt and pepper to taste. Leave the lid on till you're ready to serve.

For a faster version, toss turkey sausage pieces into skillet, cabbage on top, then cover. Over medium heat, occasionally stir until sausage is brown and cabbage is tender.

Fried Rice

One couple we know survived on this through most of a winter without serious emotional or nutritional repercussions.

1 pkg Sizzlean™
Cooked rice
Celery, chopped
Onions, chopped
2 Eggs
Lite soy sauce
Nuts—pine, almonds or peanuts

1 Cut Sizzlean™ into bite-sized pieces, then fry. Drain fat.

2 Put rice in skillet with Sizzlean pieces, medium heat, then add the amount of celery and onions you want, and any other crunchy veggies that haven't turned soft and grown green hair yet.

3 Make a nest in the rice mixture and scramble each egg separately. You're after chunky bites, so pull bits of celery and bacon into the egg as you scramble. After each egg is cooked, stir into the rice.

4 As you cook, occasionally add light sprinkles of soy sauce to mixture.

Nuts are optional, but they add an exotic flavor, particularly pine nuts. Add last so they stay crunchy.

La Tuna Melt

An insta-dinner most kids love. A last–second lifesaver–type lunch for company. Or supper. Real basic, real good. And you don't dedicate more than a few spare brain cells to the whole process.

Bread slices
6-1/2 oz can tuna
Blop of lowfat mayo
1 apple, diced
Salt, pepper
Cheese

1 Toast bread slices and cut in half, diagonally, to make triangles.

2 Mix tuna, mayo, apple bits, salt and pepper and put in a glob on each toast triangle. Top with cheese slice.

3 Broil on a cookie sheet about 3 minutes or nuke on a plate for 1-2 minutes until cheese is melted.

YOUR FRIEND, THE FLOUR TORTILLA

If you haven't, up till now, been a tortilla fan, or if the only tortillas you know are those crispy corn things in taco kits, it's time to broaden your horizons.

When selecting flour tortillas, buy the ones that don't look like they were run over by a tractor. Machine-processed tortillas have little telltale tracks on them. You want the kind that are a little chubby and flop submissively in your hands. Health foodies may prefer whole wheat tortillas.

Tortillas are great to have around insta–hors d'oeuvres, lunch, brunch or supper.

Tortilla Things

■

■ Quesadillas, the Mexican grilled cheese sandwich

Put cheese and whatever else you want on a tortilla, fold it in half and nuke until warm, or cook over medium heat in your iron skillet.

If your party guests are internationally celebrated, use things like goat cheese, sun-dried tomatoes or caviar.

■ Burritos

Set out warmed refried beans, salsa, grated cheese, olives, lettuce, tomatoes, green onions, yogurt or sour cream, cooked ground or shredded meat.

Roll tortillas around any or all possible fillings to make the burrito of your dreams.

■ Road Food

Spread peanut butter on tortilla, roll it, and you have the perfect commuter food. Keeps for days, sealed up, and can be eaten in the car without getting any on you or your fellow travelers.

If skinny is a concern, you can glue a tortilla together with as little as a teaspoon of peanut butter.

*Wanda turns leftover
tortillas into cool
earrings.*

Sans Utensils ■

Tear off bite-size pieces of tortilla to scoop up
your dinner in bite-sized pinches.

Handy ice-breaker at adult and kid functions,
and there's hardly any cleanup.

Chips or Salad Crispies ■

Spread flour tortillas on a plate and nuke on
high till crisp, but not brown—a minute or two.
Use as chips with dip, or broken up over salad.

21

Mexican Chicken

Throw this baby together using one spoon, two pans and a knife. Beeg bonus: you don't need utensils to eat, so you don't need to coerce anybody into KP. This feeds 2 or 3: multiply accordingly.

Lowfat cooking spray
1 small onion, chopped
1 can chicken, drained
1 small can black, pitted olives, drained
Salt & pepper to taste
Ready-made salsa
Tomatoes, chopped
Head lettuce, sliced thin
Grated cheddar cheese
Sour cream or plain yogurt
Tortillas

1 Spray skillet (or use real oil if you're a marathon runner.)

2 In skillet, cook onion over medium heat for a couple minutes till soft, then add chicken meat.

3 Heat another skillet or griddle for tortillas. Warm each one, a few seconds on each side. Experienced tortilla flippers do it by hand. Keep tortillas warm by covering with a towel or napkin nestled in a basket.

Create Dagwood burritos with tomatoes, lettuce shreds, grated cheddar and sour cream, or tear off bite-size pieces of tortilla and pinch up morsels of dinner. No utensils necessary.

MEATY THINGS

Maybe we should have called this Chickeny Things. This will not be news to you veteran dieters and/or budgeters: when you're looking at reducing fat, cost and preparation time, you're left pretty much looking at your basic chicken.

Fish is great (when the price is right), but because it has to be really really fresh, you can't stock it, which means an extra stop on the way home. You can freeze it or buy it frozen, but it's just not as reliably terrific as chicken.

Which is to explain that although we're just as crazy about fresh grilled ruby trout as the next person, it doesn't qualify within our very stringent parameters for FAST and CHEAP. For that you need good quality local chicken, cheap cuts of beef or pork chops.

Skillet Chicken Breasts

■

Spend the money on boned, skinned chicken breasts and you've taken all the fat calories, a lot of waste and most of the prep time out of dinner. There are a million things you can do with them—chopped in stir-fry dinners, slivered into pasta dishes, grilled, flattened, whatever. They keep in the freezer well, can quickly be nuked to defrost, and cook up with very respectable style in five or ten minutes.

4 boned, skinned chicken breasts
1 tbsp olive oil
Garlic (fresh or powder)
Tarragon
Lemon pepper, salt

1 In a large skillet, cook the chicken and garlic in oil till firm and golden all over.

2 Season with tarragon, lemon pepper and, if you want, salt, and cook another minute. Cover and let sit in hot pan.

Serve with pasta or rice, Mushrooms Melissa, Peggy's Carrots and salad.

Rick's Baked Chicken

You've had baked chicken, but never like this. And–a quality we love in an entrée–it's tidy. You can clean it up on one quick pass through the kitchen. Turn your oven to 350°, then slap this together.

Lemon juice
Garlic powder
Butter powder
Pepper
Grated Parmesan cheese
Cut–up chicken parts, (boned & skinned breasts are lower fat)

1 Rinse off chicken parts, then toss them on a cookie sheet you've spread with tin foil.

2 Dribble lemon juice, then sprinkle remaining ingredients willy–nilly over chicken.

3 While baking at 350° no more than 45 minutes, take a hot bath, pave the driveway, finish your thesis, then change into your soft clothes.

Great with rice, salad and Binky Beans.

Rick's Baked Chicken II

(Or, Son of Rick's Baked Chicken.)

Do exactly as you would for Rick's Baked Chicken, then slosh your favorite salsa over the chicken pieces instead of (or on top of) other seasonings, and bake.

If you wound up with a bundt or angel food cake pan from one of your marriages, spray it with cooking spray and shove hot cooked rice in it, then unmold onto a platter. Fill the center with Rick's Chicken, or with deli meatballs in sauce.

RICK'S BAKED CHICKEN II

Roast Chicken 'n' Noodles

_____ ■

Dieters will want to remove all the skin and visible fat from a whole fryer. Athletes, straying dieters and unrepentant Sybarites will just cut off the hanging fat blobs, remove the paper-wrapped giblets from the chest cavity and rinse the bird in cold water.

Why rinse? Because your grandmother did, and it seems like the right thing to do.

If you're a glamorous, sophisticated single-type person who may, for reasons which we'll not explore here, wish to impress someone with what a down-home, unpretentious person you really are underneath that Madison Avenue veneer, this is your chicken dish.

1 whole fryer
Olive oil
Paprika
Lemon pepper
Garlic powder
Cooked pasta—any kind
Parmesan cheese

1 Put the chicken in a deep-sided pot, rub a little olive oil over the chicken and sprinkle on seasonings. Instead of the paprika/lemon pepper combination, you can also use thyme, sage or other favorites.

(continued on next page)

2 Bake covered at 350° for about 30 minutes. Uncover, baste with pan juices and bake uncovered till browned on top, about 15 minutes. Recover and turn oven off.

3 Meanwhile, cook pasta. Any kind.

4 Remove whole chicken from pot and place on a platter. Spoon some pan juice over it.

5 Dump cooked, drained pasta in the chicken pot, sprinkle on lots of Parmesan and stir it around in the chicken drippings.

Arrange pasta around chicken on the platter and serve.

Sweet & Sour Chicken

∎

More absolute proof that your pal the Chicken Part will always come through for you. Possibly the world's best way to deal with thighs and legs you get on sale for practically zip. Good enough to hold its own at a country church supper.

1 cut–up chicken or chicken parts
1 can pineapple, unsweetened
1/4 c soy sauce
1/4 c red wine

1 Rinse chicken and toss unceremoniously in a baking dish.

2 Add large can crushed, sliced or chunked pineapple with its juice, soy sauce and wine, right on top of chicken.

3 Bake uncovered at 350° no more than 45 minutes. Occasionally flip pieces around in sauce if you have the time. Chicken should be so tender it falls off the bone.

Serve with Rice.

Pork Chops 'n' Cabbage

Pork chops are just too wonderful to reject in overzealous pursuit of more perfect thighs. We love your thighs. You'll feel the same about this straight-ahead, perfect dish which, by the way, is a legit diet item if you trim the fat and keep portions reasonable.

Lowfat cooking spray
Pork chops
Salt & pepper
Lite soy sauce
Cabbage

1 Spray skillet, season and fry pork chops, remove from skillet.

2 Whack up cabbage, toss in skillet among pork chop leavings.

3 Sprinkle with soy sauce and stir around until it's done the way you like it.

4 Pile cabbage on pork chops and serve.

London Broil

■

A sure-fire, all-purpose, Special Guest dinner suitable for everyone but your staunchest vegetarian friends. It's best to plan a day ahead because London Broil should marinate at least a few hours.

You can grab a packaged London Broil at the supermarket, but it's nice to let a real live butcher help you pick out a good cut. It makes you feel like you've really done something.

1 London Broil steak (1/3 to 1/2 pound per person)
2-3 garlic cloves, chopped
1 c red wine
1/3 c lite soy sauce
Pepper
1 tsp Dijon mustard

1 Put the meat with all the other ingredients in a deep-sided baking dish, storage container or plastic bag that will hold liquid. Make sure marinade is mixed well, then cover the dish or seal the bag and let sit in fridge at least 6 hours but no more than 3 days.

2 Broil steak very close to the flame till the edges are blackened a little on one side, then the other. For stronger flavor, stuff some of the chopped garlic from the marinade in openings in the steak.

(continued on next page)

If grilling—about 3 or 4 minutes on one side, then on the other just till juice begins to run from the top.

After cooking, let sit a few minutes, then slice diagonally and arrange on a platter. There will be medium– rare to rare slices toward the middle and more well–done slices toward the ends.

Serve with Spinach or Red Pepper Soup, Mushrooms Melissa, Peggy's Carrots, green salad and extra sour sourdough bread.

FASTA PASTA

Yuppiness has brought with it some unfortunate baggage on the subject of pasta. Remember, a noodle by any other name is still a noodle, and you can cook it any way you want. But this wouldn't be a cookbook without our own version of the Right Way.

No oil. No salt. No measuring. No rinsing. Just dump it in boiling water, let 'er rip till it's ready, empty it in a colander and shake off excess water. That's it. The one True Way.

Things Nobody Outside the Family Knows About Pasta

1 To keep pasta from congealing into a ten–pound blob after it's cooked and drained, dribble a thin coat of oil or sauce on it, just enough to keep pasta parts from adhering. Even after a week in the fridge it'll pry apart.

2 Make more than you need for one meal and keep a stash of cooked pasta in the fridge for great insta–meals such as this classic leftover side dish or main course: Combine red sauce with pasta and fry leftover glob in a little oil till crispy. (Yes!)

3 For rich tasting but skinny main course, mix pasta—preferably mostaccholi or giant shells—with red sauce and several giant blobs ricotta cheese. Adjust ratios according to taste and appetite.

Authentic Sicilian Red Sauce

The best and quickest red sauce you've ever made. The Real Sicilian Article, by way of Chicago.

Red wine
Cooking oil
2-3 cloves garlic (depending on how secure you are in your relationship)
8-oz. can tomato sauce
4 oz. can tomato paste
2 c water
Basil, thyme & oregano
Bay leaf (remove before serving)
Salt & pepper
2 Tbsp sugar

1 In a pot deep enough to keep sauce from blurping all over your kitchen walls, brown garlic in a little oil, a Tbsp or more.

2 Add tomato paste by opening both ends of can and pushing one end out the other. Smoosh around in pot to brown it a little.

3 Add tomato sauce, then fill the can with water and dump it in. For thinner sauce, dump in another can of water.

4 Add seasonings according to psychic feel— about a teaspoon each. Pour the glass of wine you're drinking into the sauce and simmer at least 20 minutes. Salt and pepper if you want.

Dump over cooked pasta topped with gobs of grated Parmesan or Romano cheese.

Mo Betta Feta

■

This will impress even a Mom from the Old Country, and you can do it without missing one word of MacNeil/Lehrer or taking your eyes off your dinner guest or toddler. Don't try it on the kids without a pre-taste test, however. Feta cheese is too much like stinky cheese for a lot of little people.

Egg noodles or fettucini
Feta cheese
Tomatoes, chopped
Butter powder
Garlic powder
Basil
Salt & pepper
Green onions if you got 'em

1 In a bowl, mix hot cooked pasta with everything else. No feta? Jeez. Go with cottage cheese.

2 Nuke slightly to warm the feta, toss and scarf. Unless it's for company, in which case you'll want to do a little more in the way of presentation. Plates, maybe. Utensils, that kind of thing.

Oya Ooya

A very badly corrupted spelling of a very, very good Italian classic. Based on oil (oya) and water (ooya), it's the perfect recipe when you've run out of time and there's nothing left in the fridge but film and Kosher horseradish.

1/8 c olive oil
1 or 2 cloves garlic
1/2 c water
Basil, big pinch
Oregano, big pinch
Parsley, big pinch
Thyme, big pinch
Salt & pepper
Parmesan or Romano cheese

1 On low heat, brown garlic in oil.

2 Add herbs and water, stir and heat till simmering. You can serve immediately or simmer for hours, it's up to you. The longer the stronger.

Serve over favorite cooked pasta with mounds of grated Parmesan or Romano.

Linguine & Clam Sauce

Most folks don't know what a no-brainer this is, and you don't need to tell them.

Add a 6-oz bottle of clam juice and a 4-oz can of clams to the Oya Ooya recipe. *Whew.*

Wanda staggers to her knees as she completes another incredible pasta masterpiece.

Spaghetti Carbonara

Okay, you're going to need two pots for this. And it does involve cooking your lower-fat bacon-type product separately, which could actually be construed as sautéing, which we, as you know, don't do. Even with that, it's soooo easy, and one that will have your subjects groveling for more. Feeds four to six Earth people.

Spaghetti or spaghettini, cooked
1 pkg. Sizzlean™
Chopped green onions
1 or 2 eggs
Pepper
Olive oil or butter substitute mixed with water or, for unreconstructed Real Food fans, "bacon" fat
Parmesan cheese

1 While pasta water heats, cut Sizzlean in 3/4" pieces and fry in iron skillet till crisp. Drain and set aside.

2 Put eggs, onions and pepper in large bowl and beat with a fork to mix.

3 Drain cooked pasta and, immediately, while it's still really hot, throw it on top of eggs and onions.

4 Add cheese and Sizzlean, then toss till eggs aren't runny.

SOUPERS ™

If you're particularly concerned about the SKINNY part of our promise, this is *your* section. Not that the rest of the book will lead you astray, but these Soupers are lean enough for hard-core dieters.

They can be a first course for company or a whole meal in themselves.

If you usually eat too fast and want too much, our Soupers automatically slow you down and fill you up like no other low–cal meal.

And every time you eat a Souper instead of one of those cardboard diet dinners, you save two or three bucks, a couple hundred calories and untold amounts of sodium. Not to mention all that stupid packaging.

Bogus Borscht

■

The thing about this souper is, even if it weren't wonderful tasting, which it is, or magnificently healthful, which it is, you should make it just to see it. The deepest, almost translucent vermillion red you see only in roses, rubies and, once in a while, nail polish. Gorgeous. Especially with a blop of nonfat yogurt on top, then a curl of orange peel.

For one serving:
1 good-size beet, whacked up
1-2 carrots
1 chicken bouillon cube
1/2 to 1 onion
1/2 c or more water
2 glops nonfat yogurt
Butter flavoring stuff
Salt
Orange peel, vinegar or lemon juice

1 Nuke beet, bouillon, carrots, onion, and water till beet is tender. You can cook some cabbage with the beet and onion if you have it, but you won't miss it if you don't.

2 While contents are cooking, put yogurt and salt in blender.

3 Add cooked beets and liquid to ingredients in blender. Blend till smooth, add seasonings to taste and re-blend.

Carrot Soup

This is enough for one person to pig out on or two people to share.

Store carrots sealed away from other fruits and veggies so they won't get bitter. (Only certain fruits and veggies make them bitter, but don't waste your time trying to remember which ones.)

4-5 carrots, whacked up
1 chicken bouillon cube
1 garlic clove
1 c water
1/2 to 1 onion, whacked up
1/4 c powdered milk
Butter substitute
Salt

1 Put carrots, bouillon, garlic, water and onion in a quart Pyrex™ measuring cup or facsimile. If you're trying to use up zucchini the neighbors gave you, put some in with the carrots.

2 Nuke, covered, till carrots are tender, 8-10 minutes. While carrots are being nuked, put dry ingredients in the blender.

3 Dump cooked stuff in the blender on top of dry ingredients. Blend till smooth.

To buff up the soup for company, add a pinch or two of curry powder or 1 packet of Equal™.

Red Pepper Soup

Worth making just to look at. Gorgeous. Makes a swell meal with corn muffins and a green salad.

2 big or 3 small sweet red peppers
1/2 yellow onion
2 chicken bouillon cubes
1 c water
1 carrot or zucchini if you're trying
to use them up
2 cloves fresh garlic
Butter substitute (cheese flavored is good)
Salt
1/4 c powdered milk

1 Put bouillon and water in a 1-quart Pyrex™ measuring cup or other microwaveable container. Slice veggies into same container.

2 Nuke, covered, till tender, 6-8 minutes.

3 Meanwhile, put rest of stuff in blender. Add veggies when done, liquid and all, and blend till smooth.

Garnish generously with grated cheese.

Smoky, Chunky Pea Soup

You will immediately recognize this thinly veiled update as your old pal split pea 'n' ham soup, minus several billion calories, a lot of salt and hours of simmering. Instead of a wispy shadow of its more robust antecedent, what you get is fresher flavor and upmarket élan.

1 small bag frozen peas
1/2 to 1 c water
Nutmeg or thyme
1 chicken bouillon cube
Butter substitute
Powdered milk
Chunks of smoked turkey breast

1 Nuke peas, water, spices and bouillon till peas are warm.

2 Put a few whole peas aside for garnish, and blend rest till smooth.

3 Add cubes of turkey breast (3 or 4 oz or more, or less).

4 Nuke, covered, on medium to low till it's bubbled a while.

Garnish with whole peas.

Spinach Soup

This is nothing but Creamed Spinach with a couple of adjustments.

10-oz. pkg chopped spinach
1 chicken bouillon cube
1 c water
1/4 c powdered milk
1 tsp artificial butter type stuff
Salt & pepper
Nutmeg, 2 shakes

1 Put dry ingredients in the blender. Go easy on the nutmeg till you know how you like it.

2 Nuke spinach till steamy, then toss—liquid and all—into blender with other ingredients.

3 Nuke water and bouillon cube to boiling, add to the blender and blend till soupy.

Garnish with grated cheese.

SCENE STEALERS

These are the reliable performers that can play lots of different roles—always convincing—and always so memorable in their supporting roles that people forget the show was low budget.

You can bring them in at the last second with little or no preparation and know they'll get a great reaction.

Rice Rice Rice

Pay no attention to anything anyone may have ever said to you about The Right Way to cook rice. You know, a sister–in–law who sniffs at the thought of the rice grains not clinging to one another, as they should in better homes.

Make it pretty much according to package directions in a pot with a tight fitting lid.

If it turns out sticky, tell everyone that's the way it's best.

If it turns out unsticky, make it a point to mention how sticky rice will ruin an otherwise glorious meal.

In any case, make a fairly large grunch and you can get a week's mileage out of it.

Rice Salad

Here's what you do with some of that leftover grunch of rice you made Tuesday.

Lowfat mayo or vinegar & oil dressing
Frozen peas
Green onions, chopped
Frozen crab or canned tuna
Canned water chestnuts if you got 'em
Capers if you like 'em
Olives if you want, sliced. Black or green
Lemon pepper, salt
We're hazy here about amounts because it doesn't matter much. A can of tuna, small or big. A half-bag of peas. Whatever.

1 Dump in as much as looks right to you.

2 Stir everything up and let the flavors blend in the fridge a while.

A great picnic item or swell for bag lunch. Leave out the tuna or crab, and you have the perfect dish for a vegetarian potluck.

Polynesian Rice

For sultry evenings when jasmine fills the air and you want something exotic. Or maybe you just want to stand at the stove and eat out of the pot.

Cooked rice
Pineapple chunks
Brown sugar
Pine nuts or almonds

1 In rice pot, stir in brown sugar, fresh or canned pineapple chunks and drops of pineapple juice to taste.

2 Stir nuts in last and serve while rice is still warm.

Curried Rice

We're pushing it to call this a recipe, but that's the point. You shouldn't have to stop and look up things or do a lot of serious brainwork just to get a meal on.

When you're running a FAST, CHEAP & SKINNY kitchen, there are certain effortless moves you fall back on. You're the only one who has to know it took two seconds and two ingredients.

Cooked rice
Eggs (1 per 2 c cooked rice)
1/2 tsp curry powder

1 Have your eggs ready so when you lift the lid off the rice you can immediately crack an egg or two onto the steaming rice.

2 Quickly stir the raw egg into the rice, and it cooks by the heat of the rice.

The egg gives the rice a buttery flavor that's terrific with nothing else on it. If you're not wild about curry, leave it off.

Put into one of your better serving dishes, shape it into kind of a dome and sprinkle curry powder on top.

Fried Green Peppers

You're scanning the produce section, and two or three green peppers leap out at you. Later you rediscover them in the back of your vegetable bin, starting to lock green hair with the now impotent celery.

Don't throw them away! Just carve around the sink holes and have the rest for dinner.

Lowfat cooking spray
Cooking oil
Garlic (fresh or powder)
Green peppers
Salt & pepper

1 Spray skillet then pour about 1 Tbsp cooking oil in to brown the garlic.

2 Slice peppers lengthwise. Dump in skillet.

3 Stir peppers often over medium heat till limp and floppy, even singed.

Salt and pepper at last minute and serve with your favorite pasta.

Creamed Spinach

Creamed spinach, unadorned, bears an uncanny resemblance to pond slime. But with a swell name like Épinard de Soie (French for Spinach Silk), plus one of your better soup bowls, and some cheese with an attitude, hey.

10-oz. pkg chopped spinach
1/4 c powdered milk
1 tsp artificial butter type stuff
Salt & pepper
Nutmeg, 2 shakes

1 While nuking spinach (till steamy), put everything else in the blender. Don't bother measuring too carefully, but go easy on the nutmeg till you know how you like it.

2 Toss nuked spinach—liquid and all—into blender with the other ingredients. Blend till smooth. To make it thinner, add a little water or milk.

3 Sprinkle grated cheese on top before snarfing. Feta, Swiss, Cheddar, Parmesan— everything works with good old Épinard.

Serve as a main course with bread and wine or on the side with London Broil or Rick's Chicken.

Binky Beans

■

This one particular family, and of course we won't mention names but you know who you are, serves this at least once a week because it's the only green thing their children will allow past their molars.

No one doesn't like them a lot, and large numbers of people are quite addicted.

Kids love to make this because it's one of the few things they can legally shove around and smash and singe. This kind of abuse only makes Binky Beans better.

10-oz can short-cut green beans, drained
Olive oil
Lots of fresh garlic and/or garlic powder
Lemon pepper–OR–
Lemon juice or vinegar + pepper

1 Put all in iron skillet over high heat. (If using fresh garlic, slice at least one clove per can of green beans.)

2 Move beans around with spatula till they brown. Crisp is okay.

This dish takes about 10 minutes from start to finish and goes with just about anything.

Lovable Limas

If your mother made you eat nasty, grey-green lumps of sandy, squishy yeckiness, this recipe will change the way you think about limas forever.

Frozen Fordhook limas
Lemon juice + pepper or lemon pepper
Butter substitute
Water, a few drops
Garlic powder

1 Nuke limas in their box or covered in a microwaveable dish for considerably less time than it says on package directions. Remove when steamy hot and barely tender.

2 In a bowl, toss beans with ingredients.

Even kids like these. Honest. Your mom, however, may still prefer the squishy, grey-green, ooky kind.

WON'T YOU
PLEASE LOVE
ME... SOMEBODY
PLEASE LOVE ME.

Mushrooms Melissa

In this dish, three strong flavors harmonize like the Andrews Sisters to create a long-standing memory. Like all war food, this doesn't take much from the pantry. Excellent over rice or London Broil or on its own.

Butter substitute or butter
Lemon juice
Soy Sauce
Dill weed
Mushrooms

1 In equal parts, put butter stuff, lemon juice and soy sauce in a skillet over medium-low heat.

2 Add enough dill weed to punch up the tang.

3 Add fresh mushrooms. As many as you want. Keep or throw away your favorite parts, it's your kitchen. Canned mushrooms? In a pinch only.

Serve immediately or simmer till mushrooms are unrecognizable.

Peggy's Carrots

Your basic "less is more" approach to The Perfect Vegetable Side Dish. No one will believe this is all you did.

1 bag carrots
Butter substitute (or real butter)
Garlic powder
Parsley
Pepper

1 Nuke or steam carrots, covered, to desired consistency.

2 In a bowl, toss drained carrots with everything else. Adjust to taste.

For variation, add honey or Equal to taste.

Ze Best Zucchini

Books have been written about zucchini. This, we feel, is the bottom line.

Zucchinis
Olive oil
Garlic powder
Lemon pepper

1 Slice zucchini lengthwise.

2 Brush with olive oil, sprinkle with garlic powder and lemon pepper.

3 Cover and nuke till tender, or grill.

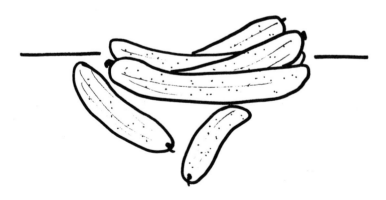

BRUNCH

It's that neither–nor category of meal. Food that seems right just after midnight or late Sunday morning, at which time not just anything sounds like a good idea.

These brunch items are fast, cheap tricks to pull out of your bag at odd times or any time. Not often, however, if skinny is a major concern.

But if, for example, it is Sunday at 3:00 and you've ridden your bicycle 30 or 40 miles and played rugby in the park and don't plan to eat again until Monday, it will not ruin your life to dive into a plate of the Best Hash Browns Ever.

Best Hash Browns Ever

This is not exactly low cal, but it is seriously divine. By that, we mean these potatoes are to be served only to people you want to keep coming around.

1 large baking potato per person
Canola or other unsaturated oil
Paprika
Garlic powder
Salt & pepper

1 Nuke unpeeled whole potatoes till just barely tender. Slice and put in iron skillet with oil, about 1 Tbsp per potato.

2 Add seasonings and cook over medium high heat till golden and crispy around edges, 5-10 minutes.

Serve with Rancho Eggs and sliced oranges.

Mexican Egg Nests

With this one-pan, one-can meal you get lotsa latitude and no guilt no matter how it turns out. One brunch item you can't ruin, especially when served with frosty cervezas.

Lowfat cooking spray
1 can no–lard refried beans
Eggs
Water
Cheese
Tomato
Onion

1 Spray skillet, then heat refried beans over medium-low. Make nests in bean glob.

2 Drop an egg in each nest, dribbling no more than a teaspoon of water on top of everything.

3 Put tight-fitting lid on skillet and steam the eggs a few minutes, checking occasionally to see when you want to stop.

Top with grated cheese (sharp cheddar is good), tomatoes in bite-sized chunks, chopped onions and very thinly sliced lettuce. Or, make little nests of shredded lettuce and onions, and put egg/bean glob on top.

Pumpkin Pancakes

Pumpkin is one of those things not everyone craves. But the people who do are passionate. If you know who they are, this is a particularly easy way to enslave them for life. Remember, get those boxes and cans off the sink and into the trash immediately.

Low-fat complete pancake mix
Regular, old-fashioned oatmeal
Canned pumpkin
Cinnamon
Nutmeg

1 Into a bowl of enough dry pancake mix to feed everybody, add a glop—2 heaping Tbsp—canned pumpkin, 1/4 cup oatmeal per person and half the water called for on the package.

2 Sprinkle in cinnamon, add a dash of nutmeg, and stir, adding water little by little till batter is still thick but will spread out from its own weight when you spoon it onto the skillet. Help it spread with a spoon so it won't be too thick.

3 Cook till edges appear firm (don't wait for bubbles as in ordinary pancakes), then brown the other side.

Serve with plain yogurt sweetened with Equal and vanilla. And/or lite syrup.

Kelly's Rancho Eggs

You've somehow ended up with everybody at your place for brunch. It's none of our business how or what happened last night, but you now have 30 seconds to come up with something, and it had better be good. Well, here ya go.

2 eggs per person, 3 if your pals run large
Margarine
Salsa
Grated Jack or Cheddar cheese

1 Beat eggs with a little water in something they'll pour out of easily.

2 Melt about 1/2 tsp margarine per egg and swirl around till you coat omelette pan or skillet, then pour eggs in pan and cook over medium heat, lifting cooked eggs from bottom so uncooked egg runs underneath

3 Add a heaping tsp salsa per person to the mixture as it's cooking.

4 When almost as firm as you want, add grated cheese and mix well, then garnish with more salsa and cheese.

Serve with corn muffins and sliced oranges. Why sliced oranges? They don't run and make the plate gooky, they keep forever in the fridge (unsliced), they look terrific and they scream healthy.

Out-of-Desperation Desserts

We know better than to include divine little recipes for stuff that would be dangerous to have lurking in the fridge.

In this section you'll find ways to put something on the table that looks great and passes for dessert when you have company, and things that will keep you from bundling up and going out in a blizzard for brownie mix because your ex-husband called or your girlfriend didn't.

Emergency Chocolate Sauce

For people with a chocolate problem.

3 heaping tsp cocoa, unsweetened
4 packets (or more) Equal ™
1 tsp butter substitute
1/8 c powdered milk
Hot water

1 Put all dry ingredients in a cup or small bowl and stir in water by the teaspoon or by the drop till the consistency is what you want.

2 Make it milkier or sweeter by changing proportions, or add orange peel or flavorings like rum, mint, amaretto, lemon or vanilla. Or put in 1/2 tsp instant coffee.

Serve over dietetic pound cake, angel food cake, lowfat ice milk or nuked pears.

Nuked Pears

Pear
Cinnamon
Equal ™

1 Quarter a pear, cut away core and seeds.

2 Sprinkle with cinnamon, cover and nuke till tender, 2-3 minutes.

3 Sweeten with Equal and serve with Ricotta Cream.

Nuked Apples

Apple
Cinnamon
Equal

1 Slice apples

2 Sprinkle with cinnamon, cover and nuke till tender.

3 Sweeten with Equal™ and serve with Ricotta Cream.

Ricotta Cream

Ricotta cheese
Equal
Vanilla Flavoring

1 Sweeten low-fat Ricotta cheese with Equal™, flavor with vanilla and stir well.

Terrific with raw or cooked apples or pears. Garnish with cinnamon.

Raspberries for Company

■

Frozen Raspberries
Powdered sugar or Equal™
Kirsch Liqueur

1 Defrost a bag of frozen unsweetened raspberries.

2 Mix lightly with a few spoonfuls of Kirsch liqueur if you have it. If not, just sift some powdered sugar or sprinkle Equal™ on berries and serve.

Great with pound cake or lowfat vanilla ice cream.